The Gates of Pearl

OTHER BOOKS BY THIS AUTHOR:

Mink Coat (poems)

black diaries (poems)

Jilted (a novel)

MUDFISH INDIVIDUAL POET SERIES #11

The Gates of Pearl

a poem

Jill Hoffman

Distributed by: Small Press Distribution (SPD), 1341 Seventh Street,
Berkeley CA 94710; Ingram Periodicals Inc.,18 Ingram Blvd., LaVergne,
TN 37086 and Ubiquity Distributors, Inc. 607 Degraw St.,
Brooklyn, NY 11217. Available also from Box Turtle Press.
ISBN: 1-893654-19-2

Cover paintings: Jill Hoffman
Book design: Anne Lawrence
Typeset in Futura Book

Copyright © 2018 Jill Hoffman
Publisher: Box Turtle Press
184 Franklin Street
New York, New York 10013
212.219.9278; mudfishmag@aol.com
www.mudfish.org

MUDFISH INDIVIDUAL POET SERIES #11

Jill Hoffman

Preface

    The Gates of Pearl has two authors. It is in two voices, mine and my mother's: mine in my traditional poems that are mostly addressed to her; her voice in my rendering of things she said on the telephone, and her voice in the journals. I was my mother's amanuensis. I wrote down her words when we spoke every morning, maybe as a way of not listening. She was dying of Paget's disease, breast cancer. The jagged telephone poems alternate with my poems to (or about) her, and with her journals — her creative writing — that she did in Overeaters Anonymous. When my mother died in 1979 she weighed 80 pounds.

    Her life is fully revealed in her journals, mine half hidden in my poems.

    Her story is a story of divorce. She went to Mexico twice, once to a clinic in Tiajuana to take Laetrile, and once to divorce my father.

    I remember as a child my mother braiding my hair every morning for school. The knots she called Nazis. I have loosely braided these three strands into a poem, and over time her unique strand (her journal) has grown fatter. It has played an expanding role.

    Our collaboration extended from the mid-1970's until today, March 17, 2017, her 101st birthday.

Pearly (Last Days) by Jill Hoffman, 2016

"She ventured to hope he did not always read only poetry, and to say, that she thought it was the misfortune of poetry to be seldom safely enjoyed by those who enjoyed it completely; and that the strong feelings which alone could estimate it truly were the very feelings which ought to taste it but sparingly."

Jane Austen, *Persuasion*

— the washing away of the postcard, my life
bore out what I dreamed Dad really did
In my dreams you were distraught and
crying and you were writing my
story and
and I live by day to day and hang
in and hang in by my fingernails
and for you to pick a different
heroine and — I don't know —
it slipped away — I had to find something to comfort you —
that you might have to leave
this heroine, and put her away
but in the dream — your tears, your
crying woke me up! — as if
you were little and I only slept with one ear —
but your tears and your face were so —
and your shoulders too
slender for this burden. Your face
was near my pillow / a horror for me — I was
bingeing — into food —
chickens — maybe ice cream cakes — into
the food and this young man who was a doctor or was
going to be a doctor asked if I could play the piano.
I said 'Not really.' There was my parents' piano
in the corner — he would teach me the chords he said.
His name, maybe Terence, was in the society column.
Safir. (Safe Fear)

There's a poem I knew when I was a child called 'The Lost Chord.'
When I woke up I said, "That's my lost chord."
But then I got up in the morning and got
a little persnickety — I got a
little angry at Daddy — he likes to
throw a bone and not be questioned.
I have an odious task and I hope he
won't make me want revenge and
then I'll have to steal —
lentils. flanken. Key Food.
Ring the bell: make friends with the butcher.
I'm in bed with a rag around my breast. . . That A emulsion that he
literally poured down my throat — and one young guy — Tom —

Book of Pearl

I have short changed the Tel Co.

I short changed Bus Co Subway

I short changed a designer in my Father's Business by getting
his job

        I did not live up to my potential

I short changed my parents

I short changed my children

I short changed a wicked Aunt and Uncle by staying too long as
a guest (even though I earned my way)

When I am overcharged in a Fruit Market — I have not been above
evening the score I stole a 25¢ to buy Food from Aunt Rose's
Purse I stole 5 pennies from my Mother's purse

If I were let loose in Nixon's San Clemente estate I would steal
him blind for not rolling back prices when he should have This
started galloping inflation along with the wheat deal When I
was bingeing 4 years ago — I would steal ice-cream from my
daughter's fridge so they wouldn't see the gluttony. I would
steal from my own refrig as soon as my then husband was asleep —

1/2 gallon of ice cream — I short changed Jerry my first fiancé by breaking the engagement I am very ashamed that I pawned his diamond engagement ring and I gave him the pawn ticket instead of the ring

I short changed my husband (even though he deserved it) with the divorce. I short changed my younger daughter in particular — Wendy — she looked like my husband's ugly family — she was like them in many ways — a different breed I was a crying — depressed Mother. I short changed her of laughter joy and the security of a loving Mother. I short changed people in the past by not having them back to dinner in my home — we used to take them out to dinner — by doing that I eliminated the fear that I wouldn't make a perfect dinner — the anxiety of overeating before and after they left I short changed my body by being a compulsive overeater. I damaged my liver — I built cancer and arthritis loneliness — isolation and the hard work of building health with the sword

CAULIFLOWER

These things that I can give you with my bare hands
are like men on a neighbor rooftop, colorful but
suspiciously small.
Take this one long exquisite slender white rose.
I throw it across Central Park to you.
It is the white snow, the red carpet, the white
cauliflower,
the plush red coach,
the white lace at his neck, your red
stays.

my breast is worse — there's no question about it —
                              bleeding all over the lot —
I need an avocado but I think I'm going to have some bedrest.
Last night I was <u>a relentless eater</u> — I wanted my food and it's
backed up on me
All those years of fasting — and I want
                    what is coming to me — and leave me alone!
I just had a dream that I slipped and fell on the ice — and in O.A.
we say the first bite is a slip/
my body is going through something — I'm
itchy all over.

She's a hard nut to crack. I also had a dream I was foraging/
I was wanting to eat flat
                          Hungarian strudel.
And corn with sparse kernels —
all not good phallic symbols for me.
Anyone who writes about me is taking her life in her hands.
Well, I think the beer-drinker better cut down his bills.

I'm letting my illness live itself out.
I'm two parts.
25¢ is haunting me.
"Would you please cover yourself," she said. This same Elaine
gave a eulogy for me that should have only been given to me
when I was dead. I couldn't listen to it.
May is painful to me — because of rhododendrons — those birthday

cake flowers that we had in Syosset — that open out pink and white —
and because I had a chance to have them again on those two acres
near Anna. Lewis — because with drowning people you have to
get away to save yourself, and them, you give them a bop and go off
someplace in your self. Talk to the reader the way you would talk to me.

May 4, 1976

I'm in a frenzy to get to the A & P — to get to the Bank — I must pay my bills — my duties are mounting — How dare I write when I am on a treadmill of undone chores Writing is Nero fiddling — my inner turmoil Rome burning — Yet I had time for a lot of vegetarian babies who want the breast — I must call my heartbroken daughter Jill. Her novel, her literary baby was slaughtered — impaled by a threat of a 5 million dollar law-suit. I'm drawn to the writing yet I'm fretful — when will there be time for me — for freeflowing serenity from one task to another. I am writing this in the bank. It took me two months to get here. Dear God — are you helping me mend my ways Are some of the paralyzing fears going? I have a chance — will I make it? Is it the writing that is starting to free me? Yesterday I wrote at 6 AM — but I succumbed to a Veg person's plea — and I gave away my 6 Am time If I can't do all I come first — Do you hear that Pearly — do you hear that God — Is this the beginning of a little self-love.

At 9 I can still keep my mind occupied

I'm still very angry at God —
my bursitis arm
is still giving me a lot of trouble
I had the most beautiful meal yesterday

I had a lot of clean-ups
after I spoke to you

It's killing me that at the A & P with my coupon

bargains
4 cracked squash in a new box for 20¢
bananas were 18¢ a pound in another store
and I'm bringing you

     and then I got a marvelous
thing for me, Bosque pears

2 lbs. almonds, no more than a dollar
My writing teacher called me a very talented creative writer.
Y'know that Judy the writer is very nice,
and I'm sure she comes there to gather material —
it's a place of baring the soul.
I would like to write the way Grandma
Moses paints. That kind of primitive.

Julia Childs was trussing a chicken for a spit, a rotisserie.
She had to bind the legs with a lot of white rope and it bothered me
a little — her treating the chicken as if it had never been alive.

It was a roast chicken 6½ pounds. I noted the time
        I was having a baby — it
        was bound up in little cords to
        keep it safe (then it ate and its little
stomach swelled) and I said, "Oh, the baby ate
and now the ribs are cracked."

I have a theme of trying to cope — a <u>leit motif</u> —

I was up and crazy all night
You and Wendy were little
We were in Washington and all your new underwear
from Christmas was white —
Dad had done the laundry —
        he was very sweet that way
but he also took the red Christmas
                        stockings
and it ruined all your —

        and it all turned red and
I was hysterical — couldn't get it
                        out —
and I had been doing a lot of blood cleaning
in the panties are a lot of raisins — too
        many are not good (undigested)
Another woman would offer her

breast — but I'm trying to cope.
Killing myself.
I need the truth, I asked him,
'Do you see any deterioration in my bones?'

I had a dream that Harriet and Mike had gotten divorced but then
Harriet decided that he should come back and Mike came back —
loving and sweet and silent — and I thought oh — I'm going to ask
Mike to speak to Daddy and tell him how nice it is to come back.

Have I the courage to share my secrets?

This is the moment of truth. What a question! I am in O.A. two years and for the last year — I have been flirting seriously with this question. I have shared some but I always felt some secrets belong to me — to be worked out as best I can. But best as I can has still left me ill — I am praying for the willingness to share my defects — my willingness for these defects to go — my defects cause my secrets — my secrets perpetuate themselves like hardy annuals in my ill begotten garden. I prayed for the courage to be abstinent. The extra food became more painful than my abstinence. Now I pray that the freedom, the glory, the cleanliness and peace and free soaring respect I will have for myself will be greater than the illgotten gain of my secrets. God knows everything so there are no secrets. Secrets are toxic.

(Daughter-of-Pearl)

MARIGOLDS

Each morning Great Birnam Wood
walks in a dense troop
and lines the corner
That is how I know everything is all right.
Another day has been dragged potted
from the dark
behind the store or under the sidewalk
and put out into the mother light.
It is Forest Hills. It is the Champs Elysées.
It is the Jungle Greenhouse at Kew.
My silver husband has left for work.
My two rare birds have flown.
How vivid the exotic bloom
of your first words in the morning, lasting
marigolds.

It was O. A. Standing in line
like a reception — I stand to

asked to speak on our
lives — a novel — like
you're going through

those rhododendrons in the window
and Daddy who doesn't need the fresh air to live the way I do
I dreamt that Daddy and I were together — I couldn't believe it —
it was so peaceful and nice — then all of a sudden he burst into a
terrible temper — a tirade — he had asked me to get dressed and go
with him someplace. 'Is that why you're angry — that
I'm not coming?'
Instead of answering me, he got into
<u>another temper</u>. <u>Such a waste!</u>

I dreamed of you and Lewis — an oddball dream — two soldiers in
Viet Nam — I think it was you and all you've gone through — but they were
lured by somebody with a hare lip
and they had grasses of marijuana stuck through their lips. . .
And another before that the same.
The high from sugar is the same as that from marijuana with
the same destructive effects.

a fish dream
a striped bass (a yellow stripe

17

pierced the fish & killed it
Yesterday I was impatient
to eat and I pulled the
bandage off too quickly —
and I saw blood in the
        clear water —
Daddy and I used to
eat in some oyster —
or the Fisherman's Net —
6 ½ years I'm on raw
        food
the bus took me past some lovely fish
                                restaurants
'No, I have 3 beautiful daughters,' I said.
a lot of confusion these days —

Sat

I cannot tolerate the lack of interest in men's eyes. It is the newest —
coldest most alienating feeling in the entire world. It brings out the curse of
self hate over my grey

I have angry feelings over a son-in-law who can't please
my daughter in bed and doesn't try to make a good life out of bed,
I hate his drinking — his insomnia — his belligerence, his combativeness,
his swings in mood, his withdrawal from his family for his 3 in the
afternoon long naps that reinforce insomnia, his never offering me a
lift home after I have cooked his dinner — his perverted taste buds —
his Mother — his taking over his wife's role (with my daughter's permission
unfortunately) His sweetness gone. My daughter's happiness gone.
Divorce is spoken of. My younger daughter divorced. Ditto me. I feel
like a 3 time loser.

PORTRAIT

Our one soul
haggles for hours
on the phone, a
golden harp
at which I sit with long curls
in the tiny living room of long ago
playing for a queen in a strapless gown
and you are pearl and coral and well.
Till the mind fills up with black sequins,
and your proud pink satin narrative running
diagonal
under the net and lace
trips up my tongue.

I cut down on my food yesterday — 4 bananas
            instead of what I'm allowed — 6
compulsion to eat everything
                        I'm allowed —
        Walking around an
anachronism

        <u>an enigma</u>
At the meeting the blood came down through the
dark second blouse and it frightened a lot of people.

            he's a married man — nothing to it —
            a nursing infant
            with two mouths —
                        I don't need him
a lot of O. A. people — I will have to get tough with them
and I gave a lot and the
nurse at the meeting very high up
Kathe, pretty, not so
young blonde girl 42 can
pass for 25
pandering to their infantile behavior
The man with the dead eyes.
I made a vow
First I come
because he
doesn't even know that he's <u>a killer</u>

You don't tell someone who can't button up
                    to get an ambulance —
                    that in itself is frightening
                    I screamed 'What?'
        He did say, 'Okay I'll pay for it.'

Behind the emptiness is cruelty

Someone at the meeting gave me
                    a Currier and Ives
Christmas ball.
'This is because you yearn,' it said.

it burns my ass

And then I had to walk home and then I had to walk
another 3 blocks for the chicken and he —

but I got another chicken that had just come
in — a little baby one — Sylvia May —
they lead a charmed life — travelling —
I can't even get navel oranges from Florida
                                    murcots

winters in Mexico and goes to Europe every
summer. I just hope I can get there with the
stuff. And don't give them junk food. I mean
it's being nutritionally illiterate. I can't
think of another word.
He's a leper that should be an outcast.

(Anna Karenina) She gave up everything for love — even her life.
I think I did the same.
He threatened me all the time that he'd take you and
give you to his mother.

Such a fussy fruit man — I would
have bought them for ~~you~~ me
but maybe not for you.

I drag my arms out of the sockets

When I'm full I can first eat
fast and diet like crazy to maintain my figure
        nipple drawn to the side where it
shouldn't be — being absorbed into the
wound — like quicksand —

I must love you if I think chicken — only
I think it's a poor sort of love — that's what
makes me cranky —

Friday

   I find my 4 yr old grandson Matthew's face in the Metropolitan Museum In the Renoirs Gainsborough like a bunch of anemones vivid angelic that you can't take your eyes off. I find him in my dream last night He is close to tears. I am near him bending over solicitously. He is looking at what he is yearning for — it is an angel food cake made with carrots (Steve's Mother made such a cake I made such a cake when the children were young. I have been searching for the lost recipe, like the lost chord.) I said — if you eat it — your parents will punish you. He cries for it — he wants it so badly. Do you want it even though you will get a licking, I asked? I look deep into his eyes for the answer — the color is changing — his eyes are dark — mine brown green. He looks like me suddenly. Yes he said I want it! I want it The dream ends I want him (Steve) I want him I will take my licking God — is this your licking or saving me from it? God — is my aloneness your licking (beating) or are you saving me from it?

DEMETER

From you I learned joy, my middle name,
goddess of appetite, at whose touch
Farmer's cheese put on a bed of lettuce
or smuggled into tomatoes in a pink and
white motif reminiscent of strawberries and cream,
were compositions of originality and freshness.
The carnations I saw in your cheeks,
the bridal showers of apple blossoms on your white hands.
Do you remember the door in the gnarled oak tree
on the way to P. S. 3
that has opened now and closed again upon us,
each in our separate pomegranate chamber?

beating on a man's chest —
I think it was Daddy
saying 'you're selfish, arrogant, self-centered'
I didn't think of it as my father until there
were a lot of ladies around the room
(O. A. members) and there was a big
box of shoes — one man's shoes like a
big rubber — and he was letting
other ladies sit on my bed and try on shoes.
I was brought up that you didn't sit
on beds. "I come first," I said.

buffeted about and overchilled
walking from the bus to get to my
house I almost didn't make it — between the two
rivers — I had an appointment but it was
cancelled — left in such a turmoil
you wouldn't want a meatloaf made in
such a way?

I would kill somebody for three dollars.

I'll say goodbye now. I wish I
could sleep but it's impossible —

— it is getting the end of the season —

You are not the center of the universe!

I'm going to make it, don't you worry
about it. We are both in
open coffins and Frank Stella is
in the dream and we get up from
our coffins and go toward life —
and Frank Stella is my 'little Daddy' —

May 18 '76 Sat

    I had a food dream last night I was at a banquet with Steve him
There was a plate of food served Everything on it was not for me, but I
don't agonize. I felt different — alone even with him there. Everyone is
eating. Everyone is married. Everyone I am sure will have sex when they
go home I am strangely relaxed with the food plate that has nothing on it
for me. Perhaps there will be something at home for me. We try, but there
is emptiness — now deep snoring — I leave the bed — I go towards an
icy box — holding out its frozen breasts and erect Penis to me. I go
towards its pleasures and oblivion

JOY

You have a mate. Quickly
the match is announced in heaven.
Dark shadows robe you.
Everyone, but the small child, knows.
But it is not like that. The summer light
leads up-river like a raft and the breeze
blowing in all night brings the sea
in its salty net and you are Heidi on top
of a mountain, and I am there too
near your shoulders, your eyes,
on the romantic slopes.

She's been having trouble with her
abstinence
her instinct is for meat —
skittles, potato chips, and liquor.
Put your money towards Rome, I told him.
Spaghetti. Don't fritter it away.
I am moving better in bed.
I took the day of fasting to cement the crack

It wakes up sleeping tigers in me.
Some people don't know how to go. So you
have to learn how to go.
I don't choose to identify with death,
I identify with life. 'Evelyn, if I'm ever on
my back and ready to go,' I said,
remind me that I want to
go with grace, without
bitterness —as if it's nobody's
fault that I'm —
and Elga's bitter.

filthy serums — the doctor I
call a charlatan
her life was no dress-rehearsal
like mine.

  dream of eating sugar.

sexual — box and all that crap
— sugar was death
crumbs —

— compounds everything else you
put in your body —
barracino's cookies — square box —
crumbs left into the papers
and even this was not permitted me —

A Fantasy Come True in 10 Years / Pearly in Starring Role

    I undress in front of the golden oval carved antique mirror
that my parents thought so old-fashioned. It was sold. Now
I have it back. Lo and behold, my skin fits. I am lithe and
taut and young. I look down on my two lovely breasts. No longer
do I have to bind up the livid obscene wounds of one. How free
I am — not ever to be in mortal terror of metastasis. I am well
and strong. And invincible. My strength returns — I run toward
the many men I should have married. I will pick the most tender —
the most loving. Heads turn to see me as I pass — like they
used to. I want my house — my garden — my children happy
and nurtured. I want — I want — I want my youth back — my
health back — my mate back — Not as he was but could have been.

VENUS

The way gold comes out in black and white
like the moon thinking of some past
assignation in a photograph of herself,
my small feet are your hands,
and the wide wide world beyond the picket fence
has delicious treats in her apron,
the jar of milk, the full sleeves, the sky
showing through and the bare breasts
glittering and mountainous.

I had bought you a bedspread — it was
gold, olive gold, it had tufting,
scrollwork, reminds me of dead sea
scrolls, but these were like the
figure 8 so that whatever the

use the bedspread — and when
you did I thought to myself
I must fix up my home, my place,
and then we put the bedspread on
the bed —and it looked nice but I said

"You're full of aspirin and I'm full
of positives that I don't want
stolen from me!"

this room is a killer — also

a big ten dollar $7.95 book

It's rice tonight, and last night it was
yams and one zucchini and one small
cauliflower — and the yam which you
eat last.
I observe these swings of mood —
there's a lot of nicotine and alcohol
in Lewis over the years —

two Florida navels
which I have to scrounge for again.
large amount of juice
¾ lb. I'm entitled to 1 lb. It's a
pleasure to talk to you.
Don't forget that the day
I dreamt this I went to
see Penny in the hospital
and she showed me her cuts
and bruises
I was in the hospital
    they took a piece of the
bone and grabbed the

I left Daddy I had been
divorced but I was
already crying sobbing
because it had been a
mistake and I already
knew it, because I had a
child, like Matthew, only a girl —
you — or me — I was a child
who needed a father.
I was in a nice
outdoor place but rain
was coming in — and I had to sop up —
but I showed a woman my
nail — but it crumbled, ashes to
ashes, dust to dust, y'know.

The dream was I was in bed with Daddy and there were other men there — and there was a Chinese man too close to me so that it almost seemed sexual and I got out of bed and I went first. Before Daddy. He was the one to be in the bed first and that was all right because he was my husband, protecting me. . . The Chinese man might be from where I call you in a Chinese restaurant.

Wednesday, April 19

I have resistance writing this — but it spoiled my day. I overcame my shyness and I asked an experienced cake baking neighbor if I could bake a Passover sponge cake with her. I wanted to bring it to my sister Harriet. I also wanted to teach my daughters a dessert for a Passover Meal. I long to leave them Jewish roots even if it is only in a cake. I was invited — we made the complicated cake. It was so light and so high, fluffy, and such good things — a dozen eggs lemon and orange peel, I felt I was in Mama's kitchen. I look for her in all good smelling kitchens. The batter was light as sea foam. I was so happy and eager as it was placed in the oven. I was to come back for it.

I cringed when I saw it. It had fallen. I wanted to run away from my ~~mistake~~ disappointment. The cake reminded me of my life. It looked so marvelous. All the ingredients correct — The effort perfect — the results a disaster.

I stoically hide my disappointment from my neighbor

Fallen Cake — Fallen Life I want to bury my mistake No — I get tough with myself — Perhaps it will taste good — Perhaps the fallen sparrow will make something of her life. My cake won't rise but I will rise out of the ashes of despair.

(Daughter-of-Pearl)

MAMA PYJAMA

You sent me out with a spoon
and your love followed me like cereal
to school.

The breeze
made love to me while you watched
and I pretended to bounce my ball

under your window, in the courtyard, near
the waterfall.
A pearl was set each year in my tail.

I held some helpless wool wrapped around two sticks,
married
to your heavenly flannel.

(Shadows)

Passover seemed a plot to get me to live in the shadows of my past. My dreams usually put me there — like Count Dracula's cape enfolding me — his fangs are regrets of past mistakes. Regrets suck my life force.

Steve was invited to my sister's house for Seder. He called for my children. How beautiful they looked. He called for me. I brought down to the lobby my heavy juice extractor Steamer My Vegetarian food — piece meal. It was heavy Steve took my bundles — Put them in the trunk. He looked so handsome. Again the shadows descended. Why did I divorce him? I longed to be with him and be back to safety, to my old secure life. *I* would be making the Seder. I longed for our home in the woods the rhododendrons like pink birthday presents out at this time. My children around me, happy. I felt alienated at the table. Everyone was coupled I was different My food was different. The cancer made me different. I longed for my Mother and Father and their Seder. The shadows of my childhood were deep upon me, like the dusk.

It was time to go home. I was lavish in my praise for Harriet my middle sister. She was a poor imitation of Momma — so was I but her efforts were sterling Hugs, kisses, sleepy children too full stomachs, not mine. I could not even dull the pain with food. I was not allowed to. My heavy bundles back in the car. Steve dropped me off — (a car pulled up beside him) He got my bundles out from the trunk of the car. He said "Can you handle them?" He did not wait for an answer He jumped back in the car and drove away.

I was stunned. I felt dumped and old and useless like those Christmas trees left on the sidewalks Jan 1st. Stripped bare Their beauty gone and unnecessary now. I felt like a race horse who is now a beast of burden pulling the heavy bundles home. My house was dark. My future bleak. The radical illness casts a shadow of fear. I feel the shadow of the wings of death. No) — Stay in the light — Stay in the light

(Telephone Poem)

LEPER COLONY OF ONE

by Pearly Yuni Hoffman

I bleed from the breast,
I stain my blouse,
My blouse offends

Her sensitive eyes.
Her sensitive eyes
Reproach
My daring to exist —
Not whole.

A person
Shuns me.
I dare to live
Out my days.

4 beat up granny apples for raw apple sauce
Samuel Johnson said whoever writes not for money is crazy —
poetry is sheer lunacy. My lunch is already late —
Red Apple has some chicken cutlets
I don't know
a sheet a sweater the blouse
quilt cover
                         going to the
                  we had won a raffle
                          a pot filled with fruit

this call was only a token call

41

Sat *Sitting next to Naomi (my teacher)*

I never want to buy anything. I never want to choose for fear I won't like it after it's bought but I grabbed at part of a dream I remembered last night. I actually wanted two things Steve was in the dream I wanted *him* to buy them for me — but which would I choose — One was a small black shiny Rols — Royce kind of car — most impressive — like a pedigreed royal family kind of car — all picture windows and shiny silver accessories. I felt immediately I could drive it. Then the other was a black shiny horse and buggy — As a child I longed for a pony and cart — My most happy day was riding in a horse and buggy with a very young Daddy. He was 23 I was 3 I loved him — I loved the horse and buggy in the dream. I also loved the era. When I lived in Syosset, I would have preferred driving to the station that way instead of by car. I woke with an empty feeling. I have neither house, nor buggy nor car nor mate. How did I ever choose to make the decision to divorce? Pearly UnPerfect — the non-achiever — who is self destructive to boot — who booted her husband out of her heart and life and lived to rue the day.

Mon

A Bed of Roses — I was no more than 11 or 12 years. I don't remember the name of the movie — I think it was called *Temptation* — it was a romantic era 1924 or 5 all make believe yet the bed was real. Was the hero Ramon Navarro or John Gilbert — I can still see the hero's patent leather hair — the garden setting in the room — But the bed! I gasped with sheer wonder. The bed was shaped like a divan and completely mantled with roses. I had never seen such lavish and fairy tale beauty. Was the heroine Bessie Love? It does not matter. *I* was the heroine. She was lifted up caressed and placed lasciviously on the petals. There was something sexual — forbidden —that made me want to look and look away at the same time. The scene dimmed. They embraced.

My bridegroom — a dashing prince — my proses nipped in the bed.

(Daughter-of-Pearl)

HER SAMPLER (1959)

The needle pierced by thread
The cloth destroyed by care,
The candle snuffed by night,
The bed attacked by sleep:

All these images are you,
Mother; and I too bear, cross-
Stitched, their likeness after you,
Now wantonly embroidered:

The needle luring the thread,
The cloth embraced by wear,
The candle licking the night,
The bed voluptuous with sleep.

Me standing on the brink of life in all its fluffy beauty

a little peppery but very nice
I bought her almonds for a gift
but she didn't want them
and the cake was dreamy
but then her daughter came
a very lovely woman
she teaches — I don't know where — and the cake sank in the
middle — I didn't say a word — I just took the cake and went —
My instinct is — I bury my mistakes
I became

       one woman was buffaloed into not smoking and she had —
I was being examined
I said to you/Wendy/to O.A. "I have ten years to live."
That was the verdict. There was a ring on my finger and it was a
blaze of beauty — heart-shaped 10 karat diamond — I should be
wearing this more, I thought — a blaze — I liked that slip I made,
'nipped in the bed.' Tell Lewis to give up his self-centeredness
get ready for new plantings — no old farmer rituals.

I figured out why I'm so cranky —
I used to have a couple of good nails on the left hand —
constantly aware of the lump under the arm — all kinds of crazy
things that I never had before — you're breathing so heavy what's the matter?

. . . And then I should have two oranges and then I call in three.

Train

What is it about getting on a train — All aboard. Waving good-bye
— finally luggage packed — finally free from hurry & deadlines & pressure
— Steve handsome — dashing — The motion of the train acts like an
aphrodisiac. In my 30's I feel like a bride. I can't wait for the beds to be
made. Steve is playing solitaire. We are alone. I am alone. It is dusk,
then evening I look out the window. Husbands coming home — dinner
then bed. How I long for the coming to-gether. A happy ending — a
sexual release. The smiling porter is back. My genitals aching. My prince
is sleepy. My glass slipper shattered — so are my great expectations.

(Daughter-of-Pearl)

"STRANGER"

Stranger,
since I was born
you have been behind me
in a beaded gown with fringed sleeves
in the chariot, whispering,
"Remember, you are immortal!"
Mid-journey, I turned around
to tell you my joy
at some trivial thing or other
and saw an old woman
talking to God on the phone
about the raw foods for her last
supper.

Slow Writing Thurs.

The pain is slow — it slowly drags its leaden feet across my body. Pain wears such heavy spiked boots. I need to have a respite — The Dr says the arthritis is breaking up. My life, like an entrenched ice - berg in spring is breaking up. Wendy's marriage over — Jill says hers is breaking. A Hitler smashed his iron fist on her novel 2 yrs in creating. I feel her anguish To-day I am slowly deteriorating — Slowly the octopus despair is stalking and circling me — moving in for the kill I feel the tentacles — my bones are being crushed to the marrow. Come and get me. I cannot stand the slow death.

I can't work the program
my shopping is complicated

I need to see if the cheese came in
raw milk cheese

I paid a lot of money for millet

I gave up a meal and I'm not happy
giving it up — the first time

the odor
I can't even place the smell, it is so ugly

unfortunately in Mexico a woman
named Mrs. Freed did me in
        a crab descended on her
        and got under her skin
        big red mucous-colored

I remember she just used to lay there

in the middle of the night I had fever and chills
and this morning I don't

I'll have to go out limping each day
and beat my way back

I hate doubling up
I should have let sleeping dogs lie

with fasting one day equals two
days because the night is a day

a foul odor that I cannot stand

but I did go out yesterday and get
my TV guide
                        and there were some very ripe Cranshaw melons,
almost
moldy they were so ripe, but I wouldn't pay $1.49 for them.

shingles came upon me when I was low
very desperately depressed —

                fighting a battle on two fronts
                one physical, one emotional

First you sell yourself a bill of goods, then intelligence takes over,
then you get depressed, then you go crazy.

Sat April 15

Why is beauty a reproach to me? Why do I look hungrily and then turn away. I passed a new green lawn with clusters of crocuses scattered here and there. They reminded me of brides' bouquets. I can never measure up to the loveliness. I want to be a bride. Or I feel if beauty and nature are there — why is life not beautiful for me — why can't I be beautiful again and young and have — Why must God's beauty bring tears to my eyes? Why do I feel unworthy & angry to even feast my eyes on the fragile blossoms. I mount the bus — I go cross town — and the bright lemony forsythia are a blaze of glory. Look — look. It's for you. No tears — no turning away. You are worthy. Drink it in. It's for you. No brooding about the house and garden you let go —

*

Once in Florida on my Vegetarian Aunt Rose's estate I saw the most sexual happening. My eyes were riveted on the huge banana trees. You could actually hear the banana palm leaves unfurl. It was not the wind that gave the sound — the town was called Zephyr Hills and there was always a breeze playing thru the lush foliage.

Lo and behold thru the dark purplish large leaves right before our eyes like a birthing came the stalk of bananas. It was as if I were witnessing an overt sexual act. I had seen Nature's unabashed sexual blaze of glory —

an erection.

I was married, my two young daughters near me. I picked the infant up. Dear God, why not joyous sex for me. I hungered so.

NEVER-NEVER-LAND

One leg that was supposed to have come off
at the hip, began oozing its own story in wet
syllables on his trouser as he talked.
Silent between walls edged with broken glass,
followed by dogs who lurched in front of us,
she hid behind her 'book of unorthodox cures'
and let me get in bed with her to warm her.
In the next room a woman without hair lay
with her husband from the Midwest, her cough
flushing all night past the water-cooler.
Someone who looked like my dead father-in-law
questioned his fellow-sufferers with a notebook
as if he were Dante, or Jack Anderson.
I said a quick goodbye to her in the drugstore, holding
a washcloth with an ice cube to my head; she was running
to get a ride home from the clinic, her punctured arm
still bent upright at the elbow like the others.

Privacy

The phone rings and my heart jumps. It is an inexplicable fear. Privacy was thrust upon me with the divorce. Steve snored. One drawback of marriage. At first I enjoyed the heavenly quietude at night. Now the silence is thunderous and reproachful. What is it that I fear — well, you enter and see me as I am. In tattered clothes and tears — in disorder so unlike the woman who got lost somehow. Privacy. I take the phone off the hook while I eat — I am a secret eater and abhor conversing while performing the sacred ritual. Privacy means I can go out and join the throng and come home and rest my nerve ends — Privacy means — I do not have to smile — keep up a brave front — change bed linens every week like Momma said. Privacy means that I don't have to go in a room and shut the door.

Privacy means no one to help me on and off a bus — at a Dr's desk waiting for the axe to fall — at the bank overdrawn   Privacy is painful loneliness — getting up in the dead of night and trying to shut a window that won't budge is damp and corroded   Privacy is loneliness and bitterness I am Kathy on the Moors I long for Heathcliff

Daily Writing

Some one dear handed me a bouquet of white daffodils. They were like ethereal bridesmaids preening and waiting to be admired. I loved them and couldn't wait to take them home to plunge them into water. I loved them and put them on the table and drank them in while I ate. I didn't even mind too much that their beauty pointed up the shabbiness of how I lived. I cared for the daffodils, kept them cool and out of the hot sun. But despite all — they began to wane. So did my interest. Just when the flowers needed freshening I withheld my nurturing. What is the use. They will die — just when my symptoms are galloping away — just when I should be more zealous — my interests fade I desert myself. Suddenly I put my flowers in cool water and whispered, live as long as you can. Don't give up. I looked in the Mirror at my withered image — I took my hand — I waited too long for this — "Live as long as you can."

FINAL SALE

This is no time, lady, to mourn,
for years that time fashions
one can't return.

Time knows the merchandise
that never fit
was worn.

This is no time, lady, to mourn.

Mon.

I dreamed again. It was Eve that entered it. She spoke of trying to 'let go' of her sweetheart She told me his name. I knew that it would be unrequited sexual love. <u>He</u> looked to <u>men </u>for comfort. I saw her tears. I felt so sad for her She had so much to give. I embraced her and comforted her. "I feel for you" I said — I woke to fog thick — all grey — like my hair — my hair was age — age was no hope no hope of his coming back — he found comfort in golf — food — work — gambling — not feeling — not communicating not touching — not sharing — not living in bed or out of bed — Running from one business deal to another — busy — busy — running — running from his Mother — running from me I was his Mother. One and the Same

(Daughter-of-Pearl)

ANONYMOUS

Your name on the tips of candles in strange
churches, on the lips of overeaters
all through the city who want to diet down
to the synagogue of your size
wherein reigns a Pied
Piper, an eater of platonic roots,
a sacred wafer
who will feed multitudes with her wit and tears
and leave them some skin,
I surrender these unguarded words to your
ear that is small and tender
and apt to forgive.
Ever have I been the jewel hung there.

May 22, Sat

A dream, a bad lover, crept into my bed last night. I awoke in despair, nausea like the moment of a horrible truth. I was talking to him about a gossipy friend whom he detested — Yes he could not abide her heavily painted face Yes it nauseated him — yes, she was crafty and manipulative. I was peaceful — at least we agreed on something. Our values were always different I never felt he was my friend but now our conversation was friendly. Oh how I longed for love safety coziness Then suddenly I remembered something she said and I asked him "Who is Martha? A long pause Some woman "Do you like her" The fear choked the other questions rushing to my throat — a long Yes. No — this wasn't happening Are you serious about her Well - she's nice, comes from a good family. We have an understanding. Pain and disbelief. This is it — I thought — this is how you feel when you know you are going to die. "What is her name?" I asked. I had to know before I left this earth. Martha Selback (or Set Back) Martha Who is she What is she? Martha Washington — first lady — Martha a friend who returned to school — College — something I should do — He set back — my warm loving and gorgeous youth — He who helped Set Back every need, all normalcy — I long to go back to him anyway — I am set back at every turn — Selback my youth to me —Selback my hopes selback my health and energy I awoke, the nightmare over now the day-mare begins

PEARL

Pearls in my ear and on my
cheeks, I have no shopping list.
My wagon is finally hooked to a cart in Key
Food. They are all calling me 'Mother,'
and rushing off into the forest

to their hurried pursuits.
It is still. I am alone here
except on Thursdays when Irma
cleans, mothering the silver and brass,
mothering the brass and silver.

Friday April

   When I married I could not wait to get him into bed. I could not wait to get into bed before marriage but Steve was too honorable or so I thought. I was hungry for sex — a juicy peach of a young woman eager to love, eager to be loved. On our wedding night — he told me I was tired after the huge wedding. I was disappointed but nice brides didn't say so — I knew I was hungry. I did not know I was angry. Who could be angry at Rhett Butler — not this Scarlett O'Hara. He said — When we get to Havana — you won't be so tired. When we got to Havana <u>he </u>was tired. All my life — except maybe one or two times when there was love play — it was kindergarten stuff. I never graduated. A pox on his soft flaccid penis — A pox on a man who sought to cure himself in marriage I had an analyst who said he married a Patsy.

ELEGY

a little thing like poison ivy
magnified
and spreading under *her* mother's breast

her style grows
terse and wild as Emily Dickinson's
showing in her shriven clothes

like the inside cricket in *his* house
she sings
screaming of a bride

May 21, — Home

I was rushing to the station, hobbled by the pain the limbs — weighted down by a heavy bundle — I gave side-long glances at the antique shops on 3rd Ave. The store owners emptied their wares on the streets for all to see. The wares gave a holiday look to the avenue I wished I had time to linger I had given away better than they were selling. Still I wished I had time to browse. No — never buy an unnecessary thing again I want an uncluttered life Yet I hang on to everything All my possessions had meaning for me. Everything tied up to Mama Daddy — youth Hope. The things I gave away were (w)rested from me by a doting sister who was in from Calif. Her mission was to save me from myself — the hoarder — the Collier sister. My other sister yelling and beseeching — "No one wears that any more" — "But it's brand new," I cry. It's like my life — I never lived it — it happened — and now it's old. Outdated — to be discarded?

Push on Pearly — see the sun — feel it on your back — Enjoy the day. My eye caught the next store's wares — a table and chairs — it looked naked in the street — like puppies waiting to be taken home — it was a low table — low enough to eat on and not block the view — comfy seats — Why don't you stop and ask the price and look at it —

Don't rush by — Don't close your eyes — Don't close your mind — I don't want to furnish my flat — why are you like that? — why can't you start to live — unpack your cartons — put down rugs — put down roots — make it pretty — finish what you start. Is this my home — this boxy cubicle with urinal elevators? — Enough of that — You are afraid — Afraid to furnish — afraid to be alone and afraid to make decisions for a single life. I think of home — where is my home — and out of the blue the thunderous lightning thought — Home is where the cemetery is — where Mother and Dad are. I am just a stepping stone away. Why bother?

Sunday

I am in a bucking bronco of a subway train. I ride to the Dr. — I prop my foot up on an empty seat — a long ride — Nausea — chills ride with me. My ex-ass is riding in a fat Cadillac — a moral leper who shuns me — and my infirmities I took his parents to Drs. I nurtured them — him — The conductor came out of his booth (a train still half empty) and told me arrogantly to get my foot which was on plastic on the seat OFF I explained that I protected the seat — that even tho the seat was made for 2 — no one needed it or asked for it. That my foot was throbbing. He said No Way. If my Mother had her foot up I would tell her the same thing. I thought of all the times I was choked off trains by cigarette smoke — and conductors who said nothing. I hang my foot down. I hold my head high. I ride with the PAIN! Getting off I say quietly to the conductor who was quietly glowering at me — "I feel sorry for your mother" — All Hell unleashed. Hate spit from his mouth. He wanted my white face destroyed. I will have you arrested he screamed — if you ever open your mouth to me — My head still high — I stand him and the Pain — I was married to such violence like a sudden erupting volcano, for 32 years What is better? aloneness or being burnt by screaming lava?

THE GIRL WHO LAID GOLDEN EGGS

This girl didn't want to be told fairy tales; nobody, she said,
knew her life.
She was dressed in rags and was on a raw foods diet, had married
the wrong man and once a month
produced a solid extra large 14 karat egg that she banged
down repeatedly on the desks of chief surgeons and the heads
of hospitals
but all they could think to do was take off her breasts.
Jack carried her down the beanstalk in a sling to his mother.

And anyone who saw them never believed in fairy tales again.

Letter to a Landlord

Dear Sirs,

I could not send this check without this letter. I am sorry for the delay.

I have to tell you how unhappy I am about the elevators They smell like urinals. I can not abide the odor. I cannot abide the sickly sweet deodorants used to cover up the urine stench. It is bad for my health. I moved in here with the knowledge that no dogs were allowed (I have trained dogs — I am a dog lover — I am not against dogs, I am against careless owners) I am against the health hazard I am beginning to think, it is not only dogs but children who don't want the bother of going home to their apartments or children hostile to authority or cleanliness. The perfumed odor used to cover it up adds insult to injury.

Also — I received a stained damaged bathtub — also a cut in my brand new Formica kitchen counter top — could I please have a replacement? Also the bathroom and kitchen tiles defy cleaning. I reported the tub and kitchen cut the first day I moved in My toilet does not flush the waste down and I am constantly upset by the feces that won't flush down. HELP!

I shudder to have a guest use my bathroom

Also I have neighbors 20 G who stain the perfectly nice rug and leave heavy foot markings all over and near my door also.

Also would you please give me a rubble free piece of land adjacent to your building and mine. It is filled with dogs excrement also I want to have pride in where I live

Now something nice. I find Mr. Harrison a pleasure to deal with and most helpful, also Mr. Berwick. In fact most of your staff are nice pleasant helpful people, and I appreciate them I want to live happily here Please do something to help me. Perhaps the dogs (if they can't go can use only 1 elevator and people who are sensitive to the urine odor can use the others

Thank you — Sincerely, Pearly Yuni Hoffman

P. S. I hope to hear from you.

(Daughter-of-Pearl)

LADY AT HER TOILET

Your home-cut hair silver laurels,
one flower
in a vase

you revive in the bath, thin
Susannah
and the day trembles on its silver platter.

Early Memory (Not Easily Remembered) The Silver Brush

I loved Mr. Sokalov. I was 2 — I remember sitting with him in the park — He was a returned soldier in the first world war — mending his wounds — I found this out later. He loved me. He thought I was the smartest and the prettiest little girl in the world and said so He always had time for me — my Father — handsome — quick — never did. Mr. Sokalov took me to the Park sometimes with my Mother. He smiled at my Mother. I remember his arms the calmness — I felt safe. (Until I married him — I felt safe in Steve's arms.) I remember sun and grass and bliss in the Park. I sang songs.

In those days — people took in boarders. To get this lovely apt my parents took in Mr. Sokalov to help pay the rent My earliest memory Mr. Sokalov carried me all over the apartment. We were in his room. His silver comb and brush glittered. They were on his chest of drawers. I picked up the brush. He let me play with it all day. I left it in my parents' room. Mama 19 Daddy 23 My Father, jealous, volatile, found it there. Storms unleashed. My Mother's denials. The reproach and anger in her eyes at me — I did not know why. I knew I did something wrong. I did not know what. I pieced that together as a grown woman. I have been looking for Mr. Sokalov all my life — but on the way, I met and married my Father. I never sing songs — They never pass my lips

April 18, 1978

It was a few days before my sixth birthday. My very own day soon to be. I loved Momma so and I had her all to myself for a while. Momma loved to laugh and have fun. She smelled so good like the things she baked. I couldn't believe the day was here — the day we were going to order the cake and buy all the candy at Lofts and all the favors. Momma was all mine. My young sister safely at home. I tried hard to forget the other baby soon to come. I looked at Momma's stomach. It was big and swollen not pretty anymore. I took my eyes away — I snuggled closer. We were finally at Lofts. I can't even write the name without goose bumps even to this day. All the chocolate all the rainbow colored goodies — Momma and I discussed things and made decisions. Momma got on line to pay. I stood near her. A man was paying his bill in front of her, his valise at my feet. I let go of Momma's hand so that she could pay. Momma so heavy did not see the ground or his valise. She tripped. I saw it happening. I screamed. But I could not hear it. I did not know that my birthday would forever be ashes. I did not know that Momma's only male child would be still born. I did not know that relatives' remarks ("she had to have a party") would scar me for life. I arose out of the ashes Guilty — I had to be over good to make up for being alive and wanting a party. I could not stand Momma's grief My Daddy's disappointment Momma was very ill. We almost lost her. I thought Momma was not close to me anymore. I am afraid of parties. I can't make one without terror.

I lost my baby brother. I lost my childhood that day.

MOTHER-OF-PEARL

The fountain in her courtyard resurrected
a marble girl I believed had drowned,
Bella, who married Max when she was sixteen,
and was mistaken once for his mother.
At eight she supported a family.
She was beautiful, though her stomach rolled
over, and one toe. I was ashamed at Jones
Beach when the children looked in the window
at us naked together, taking a shower.
For years she came back, and went away
again, never having heard that my grandfather
remarried. The round horizon of the ocean
this morning is girdled with rainbow.
A blonde perches inquisitively among Dresden branches.

Sunday, April 23

I went into the fish store happily. I liked to see the large fishes swimming around in their tanks. I was holding my GrandMother's hand. I called her Bobala. It means little Grandmother. My Mama loved her Mother. I was not so sure I did. She was the beauty in the family but I felt she did not like my Daddy. She whispered to Mama that I was like him.

I was left in her care that day. I always felt alone without Mama but the fish distracted me — darting in the water. I heard the fishman and my Grandma talking in loud voices. Why did Grandma argue so about money — why was she asking how much this one cost. I was little. I hardly could see all the fish. I looked up — hoping Grandma would hold me so I could see them all. Suddenly Grandma pointed to one fish — I heard more arguing. Then the net under the squirming fish. I saw the fish open his red mouth — then on the wooden block I was shocked when the hammer came down on the head. The flailing fish stopped moving. The fishman wrapped him up in newspapers and tied the bundle with string. I looked down on the sawdust floor.

We are going to have a nice fish dinner to-night Pearly. She was gleeful. She had struck a good bargain. She had struck a sharp bargain. Grandma held out her hand — I would not take it. I could not eat.

Water

I was young and just had learned to swim. We were at the beach and it was difficult to learn with the high waves. Momma and I and my sister were alone all week and on week-ends Daddy came. That was a joy. Momma treated him like a nice guest. It was so peaceful. Daddy came on Friday late in the day. No I could not wait for to-morrow Please Daddy come with me — come with me — please. I have something to show you. Daddy looked so handsome in his white suit and striped shirt and straw hat. Daddy hated the sand — He stepped on the beach gingerly in his white city shoes.

I plunged into the water. I swam away. It was my proud moment I was doing well. I looked up to catch Daddy's eyes and to see his pride. Daddy was looking far into the horizon thinking of business. Business he always said came first. Into the horizon at the big ships so far away they looked like little sail boats, like the toys in my baby sister's bathtub. I looked up. I could not believe he wasn't watching. Daddy look at me — Look at me. The roar of the waves drowned out my voice. Daddy's gone now but I still feel the cry in my throat — Look at me Daddy Look at me.

BREAKERS

The stopping
when he was pulling on one black
sock on a chair

and she turned over
in sleep

that he has forgotten as his
face
its look of hate

is set on a pedestal
with an iron plaque: *Noli me tangere*
Don't touch me.

In the car, now he repels her, "Don't you know
I'm geared for driving
at this speed?"

When they stopped, he grew more violent.
He tells me, "I dropped off
my rider, and rested."

We had spent the week
among the green swells

75

of combers while she washed her lettuce

touching the magic
heads
she would eat

watching the inexorable white hands
of the pianist
strike ten-fingered then skip

on the glassy keyboard as if there was something sacred left.

May 26, 1978

Mama always said if you dream of "duty" or a bowel movement or muddy waters the day would have dark forebodings. That night I dreamed of the hugest bowel movement I had ever seen — It was as large as the 42nd St Billboard advertisement of a huge frankfurter — This was on my bathroom sink — it was blackish it had a crack in it — my dilemma was to get it into the toilet without the feces breaking. I could not manage this it broke. The excrement soiled my hands. I awoke with apprehension. I got up — I had to face the day — and aired my bed — my lovely puffy quilt and Pillow. It was still dark — so early in the morning I feel sneaky — like well bred people don't air linens — I left the bedroom — in an hour when I went back to make the bed — I couldn't believe it — there was an empty space where the quilt was — Disbelief — I scurried around the room It was gone. I was heartbroken My Mama & Daddy had given it to me all downy, goose down — all love all satin (my Dad had said — don't get the satin — I don't care if it is prettier — satin slides — get cotton it won't slide) — a lot of love & care & money had gone into it. I prayed that I would find it — I prayed I'd see it again — that it didn't hurt anyone — I live on the 20th floor — (My Mother's superstition — the dream — gave me a hopeless feeling) — I vowed that I would accept God's will — it would be his will if I found it — if I were to have it — Or I would let it go. I ran down feverishly — I found my tender loving Baba quilt. Thank you God it was safe — I was safe — I had harmed no one. I had back what was mine.

    This was Monday — On the spur of the movement (sic) — I decided to test God again — I vowed that if I asked ~~Steve~~ him to come back once more (I forgot that I'd be Oliver Twist again with my porridge cup out to receive gruel) I would abide by his will I ran to the phone like a 16 yr old. I had a feeling that God would find my request so reasonable that he would grant it. He was not in — I left word for him to call at his daughter's. I was rushing there for a cozy visit. I told her that I called him and why and she said, Mama — Daddy had a fight with Jack (his roommate) and he's moving. My hopes soared until she said when she saw the lights in my eyes "Mother — I already asked him" — she held me as if to give me strength — He said 'No.' I had to hear the death sentence myself — or perhaps my humor would win him — Even tho I felt like an Elegy in a Graveyard. Steve, I said thru the phone — How about us being roommates — I asked for love The "No" had the finality of an obituary. I remembered my vow. God said no. The lights went out. It was a bad day — Mama was right about dreams

DYING

When you first whispered the word in Queen Anne's
lace, there was no cry of anguish
more matter-of-fact. The unhappenable
happens. It happens all the time. It happens every day.

But you have miracles up your sleeve and shopping
carts and amazing heads of celery
ringed with rubber bands. You are a friend
to the elements and the top leaves and the bruised.

Yet you know more than we do of his table manners.
And when I came for you in hell
I had a headache.
Always you are venturing before me, naked, naked.

Leave me alone

Compulsion to Overeat — Leave me alone, the nagging deadly drive to finish a full meal and want more. When I'm full — the ungodly drive for more food — leave me alone — let me be normal   Leave me alone the feelings that I want to have my meal last forever and yet I gobble it down so quickly   Leave me alone food thoughts, leave me alone this obsession for food and my allowed food. I'd give up going to enjoyable places — Leave me alone with my food   That goes for children for friends. Leave me alone telephone — you intruder I need my food and rest. I don't need troubles that the phone brings   Leave me alone guilt feelings that I haven't furnished my apt — that I never finished my education or now that I have no job — Leave me alone the bottomless pit of despair over past mistakes   — Leave me alone — the Fears that kept me from going out of the house two years before the divorce and 2½ years after. Leave me alone the feelings of shame when our family invested also friends in Steve's fur factoring business — they invested not only with him as a lawyer but with me as honest and aware of anything not kosher — and that I'd warn them. They got huge interest and huge losses and I dug a huge hole in the ground for me. I never really came out. Leave me alone feelings that my Mama died soon after. That money that was my Father's life became lifeless. Leave me alone feelings of self hate Leave me alone feelings that it was my fault that he was impotent. His mother emasculated me (sic) and he came into marriage wanting a friendly cook — his Mother. Leave me alone the feelings of rage that he called me a Nymphomaniac Leave me alone the feelings of rage over his rejection of me after I made amends — more rage at his callousness — the unfeelingness that would want to desert me now that I needed help — Leave me alone the despair over having Cancer and arthritis and leave me alone the feelings that my life span will be shortened by despair — Leave me alone children — go free — be happy — you're pushed from the nest Leave me alone the feelings that I'm ugly that I never will have a mate — Leave me alone the feelings that I was born alone and soon it will be my time to die alone. Leave me alone the feelings of jealousy — of the have's of the world and I am a have not. Leave me alone the feelings of rage at the surgeons who operated on me needlessly — Leave me alone — you doctors in Mexico who gave me deadly toxic doses of A Mulsion — which left me with crippled legs which I have now and then said my breast must come off. I escaped from N. Y. surgeons to go to safety to other cancer modalities — Leave me alone feelings of indecision, perfections, and no compassion for myself.

MY MOTHER DREAMS SHE IS A HEAD OF CABBAGE

She is smiling
in her Elizabethan
collar of white
and green veins.

But I read that 3 Jews
mistaken for cabbages
planted
eyeless outside a window

were peed on
by a German soldier
and turned their heads
slightly.*

* *Blood from the Sky*, a novel by Piotr Rawicz

May 1978

The Car —

My Father bought his first car when I was 3 or 4 years old. I still remember the day. Everyone crowded around the sidewalk to see it. It was called a Chalmers. It was the first one on the block. It was so shiny as shiny as Daddy's eyes when he reviewed its perfections. Daddy had just learned to drive. If you bought a car the salesman taught you. The neighbors were properly awed. Daddy was so young and was already a success. We left all the neighbors on the sidewalk obviously dissatisfied with their horse and carriages. Momma and I climbed gingerly into the car — everything was perfect. Daddy was perfect. We drove to Grandma's house. It was near the beach. The smells of the sea mingled with the tantalizing smells of Grandma's kitchen pulled us away from the envy of Grandma's neighbors, even my young uncles and aunt who were no more than 3 to 10 years older than I made Daddy happy. I was uneasy. I wanted everyone to have a car. I sensed the same feeling in Momma. We all crowded around the wonderful table crowned with something special for everyone. Lots of fun and joking and talk about the car. Promises to take everyone for a ride. Dishes cleared away — when cries from the people on the sidewalk made us stop. We ran out in the blinding bright sunshine. It was not to be believed. A horse and carriage had been parked behind the car and the horse had nibbled away at the shiny leather top of the hood of Daddy's car. Daddy screamed — the owner of the carriage appeared from the next house — appalled but screaming back — What do you want from me? People laughing joking envy lessening, Daddy's perfect car was no longer perfect. There was a big gash in the hood. Even the horse seemed haughty and sorry. Daddy was in a rage. Momma felt guilty — she had pleaded for the visit — I really liked a horse and carriage better. I knew I should not tell that to Daddy. The day was spoiled.

In time Daddy mended the hood himself. He stitched it — but the car was no longer perfect. He later had to send the car back for the hood to be made good as new — After that — Daddy paid a little boy to stand on the side walk and watch his car.

Dear Steve,

When you were in charge of hundreds of thousands of dollars of the families money and you neglected your trust and my parents wiped out emotionally and financially and all of our family shocked horrified demanding their money which you guaranteed & they had trusted you as a shrewd lawyer and I not wanting to turn into a screaming shrew asking over & over — why — why — why I picked myself up — Wendy who was sub - teen — Jill 16 off to college — and was going off to Majorca where I heard it was inexpensive (this was 20 years ago) and just stay and take our child away from the devastation, you said to me — Rats desert a sinking ship You sank the ship. You cur. And I let what you said stop me from taking the first independent step.

So now I am incapacitated — really physically in need of help and you long slimy rat — You smelled the cancer and wreaked more disaster as you sank and left my ship — boring holes in the last remaining life—boat

PEARL RIVER

The eyebrows of my father's brother
writhe and swagger. In the lapel
of this catered affair he wears Marcel Proust.
This is the Hoffman Circus, a carnival of
Hoffmans sipping Hoffman. My father's sister
is the Heinrich
Hoffmann whose face is *Struwwelpeter*, whose silence
fights down grim waves. "I can't
hear you," she says, pink-cheeked
Uncle Eugene vanished from her side.
We struggle for words
that are fast served on a plate with two pills
like the ceremony itself
under the thumb of the State of New Jersey.
I sit next to the first cousin
who pulled my braids and changed me to a woman
as a bell is pulled, swinging
among its pealed chimes
on Sunday until my mother saw us from a window
rolling in a ball on the closed-in porch.
Their chicken farm
was on a river with my mother's name, Pearl River.
I dance before them; the gypsy torches flame.

Requests for Love

Fear of being alone has made me a beggar. Fear makes me forget the person I once was — no beggar — Me — Fear makes me worthless, no self-esteem, no backbone so warped emotionally that I would beg to be taken back — I told him I loved him still — I overcame fear enough to ask — Do you miss me — a long pause — "Well I certainly don't miss carting you around." I crawled back under my rock only to emerge long enough to ask Do you love me — lightning struck — a sudden storm — thunderous answer — "Don't bother me." Love was always a bother to him — I feel like an old tree being planted without roots — I am prey to the elements — outside and I am prey to my own self-hate. When I am rejected — I turn on myself with annihilation in mind. No — this time I have a request of myself — No more tin cup out — love yourself. You are loved Put down roots The tree will stand firm with roots it might even send forth flowers

Sat
Looking Inside Myself
    I went to my daughter's and plucked a chicken carcass clean to make

chicken salad Everyone loved the salad That was the daytime residual I also had a lot of cleaning up after a worsening breast which I hope is darkest before the dawn of recovery

I dreamt that my breast was bleeding again — Darn it more cleaning up — I looked at the floor — more scrubbing up I did it and then I suddenly found myself looking inside myself — I looked so empty inside much like the chicken carcass, much like I really feel I saw a lot of red red blood inside — with lots of white bone and pure white fat and white bits of gristle — I said I know what I'll do — I'll jump up & down and get rid of the blood that way — then I will have no more bleeding of the breast and no moaning at the bar. I jumped up & down and the blood stained the floor. Then I said, I know I will put a bowl under me — then I'll jump up and down and then I won't have to clean up. I did just that. I awoke. I had two ways to go with the dream. I had the chill clamminess of corpse like death but no! The blood was bright — the whiteness of the meager fat & gristle was like those choice meat boutiques on Madison Ave where I used to live and in which Jackie Onassis shopped. It was a meat-eaters Paradise. Not for me this Paradise but neither will I see death in this dream I will see health in this. I see myself finding a way to cope — finding a way to live without the clean-ups I will outwit stalking death doomsday medical reports and my imminent exit date. Excelsior!

UPRIGHT WAVE

Bebe thinks of you in your Chinese green coat.
And the many examples you set Harriet
are hand-me-downs she still wears in her rough fashion.
I grew up in your closet.
Honeymoon pearl grey satins that were living
featherboas
whispered in my ear behind the loveseat.
When you talked to anyone I watched your eyes.
Those hazel upright waves
into whose depths I would fling
myself, marveling at your green knitting.

Fri

This exquisite day — with the jonquils and tulips so perky and the hyacinths sending out their perfumed calling cards the cherry & apple blossoms the forsythia — all so painfully beautiful — I feel unwanted their beauty is not for me My life is empty and their beauty is too painful for me Life rejected me — beauty is for others — my mistakes robbed me. Old clothes for me — Sack cloth & ashes. When my husband was courting me I thought his silences were intriguing — he cut out my heart with his silences.

PERSIMMONS

Nothing but trudge, and in the end
the hills steepen and the people
sharpen and stand out
like jewels magnified under low tide;
beside parsnips, figs, the Korean man
at the cash register in wet gloves
is making inquiries after you (Gloria
sends regards) in his language that is
half scissors and half lettuce spines
as he puts the produce in a plastic bag
(you are the very person one is tempted
to tell of one's passion for such mandrake-
men, bedded in lettuce and cabbage leaves).
People miss you.
Pathological fractures appear in the sidewalks.

Terror never Ending

The terror is relentless. I can't believe that I took my own hand with the help of a shrink — and put myself into the plane that took me to Mexico and into a divorced state and into oblivion. I wake in terror as if I'm dreaming of someone else who made a dreadful error — and the terror never ending that is my life and it's my neck on the guillotine. The terror that I took security away from my children by the divorce — it was an asset for them to have parents to-gether — that they had terror never ending when we quarreled — this brings back the terror of my childhood of my parents' quarrels — I am still terrified over confrontations — I shiver inside Terror never ending is the bleeding of the breast — the deep scabs the washing out the blood stains from night clothes — sheets — pillow case — Terror — I live with the sword of Damocles over my head — the pain in my limbs and the effort I put in just to make them move — Is it bone cancer? The pain in my heart when realizing I am alone — no more red carpet treatment — no help — the terror Dracula sinks its teeth into my jugular vein

Sat Feb 18, 1978

The tool of Memory — ill-used is making me anxious. I remember how much better my life was. I feel jealousy at Steve's good rich life without me. This is eating at my vital organs. It is bad for my health. Once when I was an out patient in a hospital in Mexico a lovely woman about my age found me near the sea and suddenly showed me her breast. Mine is now similar She is long gone. Another woman asked me to feel her hard breast Mine is now similar. Betty is long gone too.

When the bus doesn't come for a half an hour — and then I can't climb up on it because of heavy bundles — When I am dressed and have to turn back like this Wednesday to repair myself with time running out because of an appointment — I had the scary feeling that life was also running out —

Monday April 12, 1978

I woke angry I had unwelcome visitors — Pain and chills in my limbs. Walking would be painful — I am too proud to accept help. I don't trust other people's vegetable and fruit shopping.

I am angry at myself for undertaking this writing course. I am angry at people who sit smugly in their healthy skin spouting, "Well we all are on borrowed time" — Drat their insensitivity — Drat their inability to face another person's standing on the brink of disaster. Do they have a large node under the arm — which spells metastasis? They don't sit in pools of blood — like a whale with a fatal harpoon — Are they in double jeopardy? — I can be hit by a truck also. Get up girl — put one painful

foot in front of another

SORROW

It is a bitter cup
but we drink it gladly
in our penitential
rags
that we never change
for company.
And yet the light
comes in in a way
we like
and just the unfractured
mind
with its dish of words
can get up when it wants to
and dance.

May 23, 1978

Steve was a lie. His whole body was a lie. When he courted me —
he was reserved and ardent. I thought his reserve would fall when we were
married. Later the lie came — he feigned passion — he feigned sexuality (I
thought all men were sexual creatures. With this body — I thee wed.)
There was no warm body next to mine — just an inept withdrawn — don't
touch me kind of man — Yes he did kiss and then fall asleep. His snores
confounded the felony. He looked like my dream Prince like the Rhett Butler
so in fashion. The lie of him — ruined my life — my disappointment was
my horror and his — when my expectations withered — his scorn for me
blazed forth. I thought marriage meant undying friendship. Everything was a lie.

I sold myself an even bigger one. Things would get better. The erection
the fulfillment would come. How did I get pregnant? How did I stay so long
in my cocoon frozen in fear

When my baby was 6 mo old — I said we must part — she will not
grow up with this quarreling

He said — If you go I will have you declared an unfit Mother How
can you do that I asked in disbelief You know of my political connections —
He was Sen Wagner's right hand man — I will lie and you will lose her. I
stayed. Shame kept me from running to my parents. I died many times as all
cowards do. I hated him and my hatred is a knife that I swallowed along

with the big lies.

I have lived with this knife I swallowed — every turn my body makes —
I am aware of hurting — hurting is despair — I am betrayed — where did
the dream go — I keep the baby perfect, the ruffles, the white shoes —
my home a show place — everything in place — I am for perfection
because I am hiding my imperfections. If I were really beautiful — if I were
really special surely my femininity would make him a whole man — See I
am also buying his big lie. I want to scream — it's not true. Mama Daddy
Save me — my unspoken words were knifelike within me Why was I so
unhappy? Where did my dream go — If only my life were not so painful.
Why could I not break from my Kafka-like prison. I cannot run free from the
pain. People think I have everything. I run to food to cover up my loss of
hope. Soon my trousseau is unwearable — My hips swelling. Nursing is
over My lovely figure done with I cannot pull the knife of despondency out.
I lose hope. Every day is funereal. I build another prison with sweets and
food. I begin to hide. I am unable to leave. I cannot vomit the knife. The
knife festers. I am doomed I feel the metallic oxides spreading in my body.
I must not walk away from myself

*

I heard a new report that was bitter irony to me. Mrs. Ford had a head
cold, mind you, and could not go to Queen Elizabeth & Prince Philip's luncheon
I once had a rare head cold, no sense of taste, temperature and a

week-end at a posh Catskill hotel. Steve is a golfer — he'd kill anyone who got in his golf way. My heavy cold got in his way I begged to stay home. I imagine a thousand delicacies and no taste buds to eat with — chills fever, Steve thru a fit — he wasn't comfortable with me not there

I went — but I was ill — I had to dress and be on view. Why could Mrs Ford stay home and not me Why am I alone now. Why can he go all over by himself now? There's no wonder I feel the fool There was no compassion. I knuckled under to a temper I sold myself out.

Ballet Class with Orange Suit

in the pits of despair
but I wouldn't let myself give
in to it.
It was the suit that I bought for the
last weekend that I spent with Dad,
that we went away together.
That weekend I was sick
and he wouldn't let me alone,
it was as if he couldn't go by himself,
and when I got there —
but
      he is a shallow person who could have been of
service to me, and not
go home and take a hot bath
— where all hell broke loose —
and I feel like a bloody
                           fool

"So that it was a pleasure not to take my
      eyes off her for one minute."

It was as if
I couldn't taste anything, I couldn't smell, I couldn't
eat (which was the 'whole thing' after all)
one bloody red flag —a lifetime washed away —

May 30,

Dear God — I am pulling the knife out. Something is happening. I was
fasting and it is over. Now it is thimble spoons of food. Clarity has returned
— a Blessing — Serenity with it. I am letting go of the knife — I am in
blue water clear swimming and loosening its sharklike edges. I see blood I
am used to that — my bath water is always bloody. I tell my self — my
breast — "you are going towards health" — now I murmur the same —
I feel the silken waters buoy my body. Why give this man room in your heart
and head — <u>rent</u> <u>free</u>. Face it — You plunge the knife deeper when you
don't. He does not want you — you and the years and memories that went
before. He does not want you, your cancer, your thoughts, your sweetness,
your essence, your strength, your frailty — YOU. Face it. Swim little fish
— you are a Pisces after all — It is not so bad. You will never have him
back — this dark changeling Prince — no more reunion fantasies. Pull the
knife I can't — then Vomit it Give it up. Why are you afraid? The loneliness
— the never having anyone. You never had him. Pull. You will never have
him back. Pull. Mama Daddy the waters run red I am pulling Help me.
God let me go free.

A dream I had — I saw dazzling blocks of ice in a rushing sea —
brilliant sun — blue water — I had come a wrong way and I said If I had
not come this wrong path I would never have seen such a glorious sight The

blocks of ice were breaking up. I felt the ice berg of despair so deep inside break also Pull — pull — You will love again, I promise you. There will be healing where the knife is. We are here with you. I pull the serrated knife with a Herculean thrust The red water does not frighten me. Shades of Ingmar Bergman — knife in the water. Let it lay on the bottom of the sea with my agony.

SCARAB

I am Yuni of the royal blood.
The Nile is my hair.
There are pearls strewn in it
and delicate combs wrought with asps.
At night, by your side,
I bestow my favors.
The bridegrooms of evening grow weak-kneed
at so many slaves, human fireflies.
Please accept this little nothing,
this pin, these faience beads.

Honey — did I disturb you — split peas
one of my ten cent cucumbers
"I don't mind being disappointed for ten cents."
You must give up self-pity the way one gives up drugs —
Now are you going to Key or Daitch — look at the
chickens — give it up for I think
the wallowing builds and engulfs you —
devastation — makes me a wasteland

he has his bunk — he has a house
              down there and a family — he knows
              where to go —
I should have rubbed her nose in it.
They're eating junk foods —
              you better start looking at the food
                  you're eating —
I had to get that in but I still have —

snacks for Lewis? I'd like to
bash his head in with his junk food —
And how they wooed me!   the Beech Nut
people . . . And I didn't want
any salt used in your foods.
I was ahead of times, so
what did it get me?

Get up out of your coffin and move your feet! —

ACKNOWLEDGEMENTS

Many of these poems have previously appeared (some in slightly different form) in the following publications:

The New Yorker, The New Republic, Partisan Review, Paris Review, New York Journal of the Arts, Community Review (CUNY), *Northwest Review, Helicon Nine, Lush Landscapes Catalogue* (Box Turtle Press), *Cover/Arts New York, The Starving Artist Cookbook,* and *Mudfish.*

With thanks to the long-standing members of my Mudfish Writing Workshop, including Doug Dorph, Stephanie Dickinson, Alice Jurish, Robert Steward and Anna Halberstadt. And especial thanks to Dell Lemmon because of whose passionate dedication to poetry I took this poem in its myriad versions out of the closet and began working on it again.

And further thanks to Jennifer Belle, Matthew Schwartz, Liz Singer, and Jack Herz for their support and to Anne Lawrence for her inspired graphic design.

Jill Hoffman is the founding editor of Mudfish and Mudfish Individual Poet Series. She has a B.A. from Bennington College, a M.A. from Columbia University, and a Ph.D. from Cornell University. She is a Guggenheim Fellow, and has taught at Bard, Barnard, Columbia, the New School, University of North Carolina and in the Master's Program at Brooklyn College. Currently she teaches the Mudfish Writing Workshop in her New York studio. She is also a painter.

Pearl Yuni Hoffman attended the Pratt Institute and worked as a dress designer for her father's Blue Bird Dress Company.

MUDFISH INDIVIDUAL POET SERIES

#1 *Dementia Pugilistica*, David Lawrence

#2 *black diaries*, Jill Hoffman

#3 *Too Too Flesh*, Doug Dorph

#4 *Skunk Cabbage*, Harry Waitzman

#5 *Husk*, Terry Phelan

#6 *Marbles*, Mary du Passage

#7 *Fires in Sonoma*, Terry Phelan

#8 *Rending the Garment*, Willa Schneberg

#9 *Vilnius Diary*, Anna Halberstadt

#10 *Single Woman*, Dell Lemmon

#11 *The Gates of Pearl*, Jill Hoffman

Praise for *The Gates of Pearl*

This is a story of family and grief, a mother/daughter saga unlike any other, ambitous and relentless."

Philip Schultz, Pulitzer Prize winner for *Failure*

Decades in gestation, the riveting, poem-memoir *The Gates of Pearl* is woven together from a mother's Overeater's Anonymous journal written in the 1970s, mother-daughter telephone conversations, and the poet-daughter's exquisite verses. . . .And here is the mother-daughter relationship with Pearly confessing her most private self to her grown child over the telephone. No attempt is made to prettify the mother's fragments and idiosyncratic stream-of-consciousness. Too much of Pearly's shimmering originality, her lyricism, and transgressive voice would be lost. Taboos of silence are broken. *I leave the bed — I go towards an icy box — holding out its frozen breasts and erect Penis to me.* The daughter responds in meticulous, impassioned verse that provides a counterpoint to the mother's flying-off-the-shelves imagery. Chiseled, Sappho-like in places, unscripted free-style in others, *The Gates of Pearl* is an impassioned lament of dark beauty. It is also a celebration. Listen to Pearly: *My eyes were riveted on the huge banana trees. ... Lo and behold thru the dark purplish large leaves right before our eyes like a birthing came the stalk of bananas. I had seen Nature's unabashed sexual blaze of glory – an erection.*

Stephanie Emily Dickinson, *Heat: An Interview with Jean Seberg; Girl Behind the Door*

"*The Gates of Pearl* is a brilliant mother-daughter narrative – an epic of the interaction of two women who love each other, criticize each other & both are mortally courageous! A must-read!"

Erica Jong, *Fear of Flying; Fear of Dying*

There is no other poem on the face of the planet like this one. This is a poem that will blow the top of your head off. This is a poem in which the past is present and the present is in the past, because this poem makes the past seem so contemporary that the present feels less immediate. This is a poem written by the poet's mother in her journals, and the poet and her mother in telephone poems, and the poet in her mysterious, lyrical poems. All the voices, past and present, mingling together in this book-length poem creates a sound as piercing and clear as a scream. This is not a howl. This is a scream —a fantastic, feminist scream grounded in eating disorders, sexual frustration, divorce, failure, the difficulty of motherhood, profound disappointment and despair where the only hope is the truthfulness of the narrator, the goodness of her daughter, the determination of both of them, and the beauty of poetry. You want to read this poem despite its hard truths, because it is unlike anything you have ever read before..

Dell Lemmon, *Single Woman*

I have read your extraordinary poem. It is utterly haunting. So much pain within one tiny person! Pearly's voice is so strong in it, I can hear her speaking . . . . It is shocking, lacerating, devastating, heart- breaking, a perfect portrait of terminal longing. I don't know how you survived living it or writing about it. You have written a remarkable testimonial to a ferocious spirit doing her best to come to terms with some of the hardest realities life provides. Through your poem, that spirit lives. It's a splendid piece of work by a fine poet.

Karen Tweedy-Holmes, _Thought to Exist in the Wild;_
Horse Sanctuary

Box Turtle Press